Can you find
all of these objects
in this book?
You will have to look
very hard.

This book belongs to:

. . . .

. . . .

. . . .

Age. . . . .

© 1991 Grandreams Limited

Telling The Time written by Anne McKie.

My First Rhyming Picture ABC, My First Picture Book of Numbers written by Brian Miles. © 1985 Brian Miles.

Illustrated by Ken McKie.

This edition published in 1997

Published by
Grandreams Limited
435-437 Edgware Road, Little Venice, London, W2 ITH

Printed in Hong Kong

FL1

my picture book of
LEARNING

Have fun with

Numbers

Telling the time

Rhyming ABC

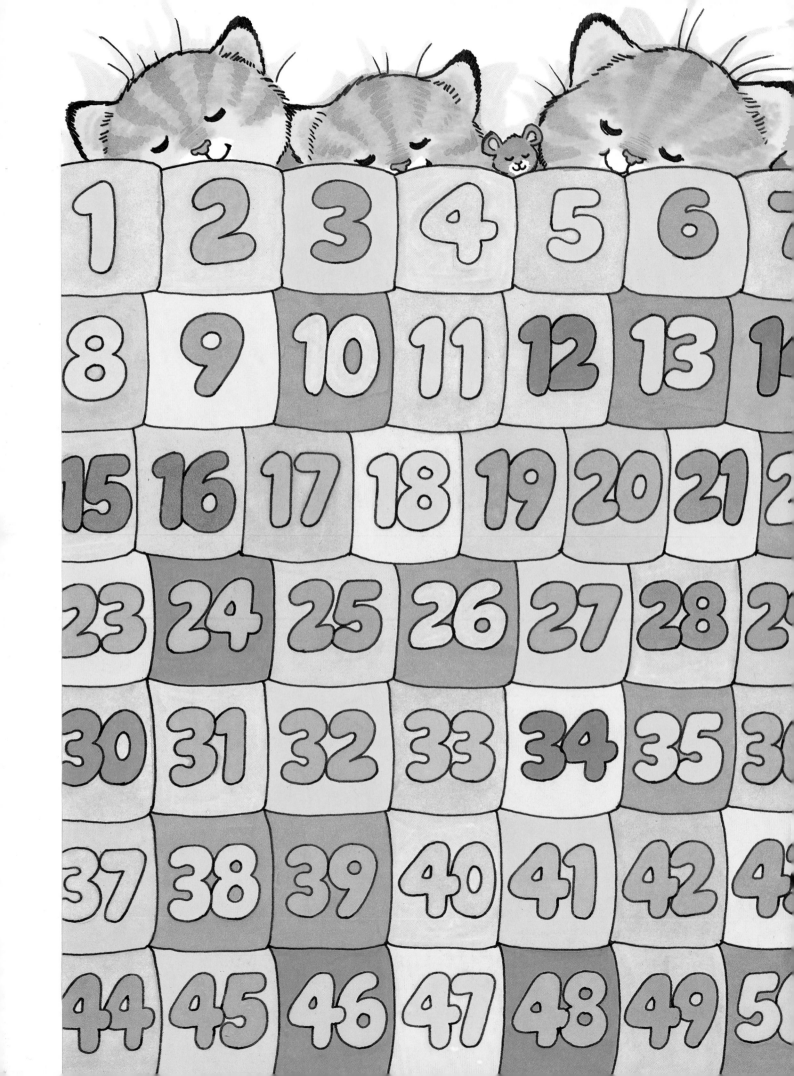

my first picture book of numbers

this is 1~one

one currant bun

1 2 3 4 5 6 7 8 9 10

this is 2~two

two red shoes

1 **2** 3 4 5 6 7 8 9 10

this is 3~three

three birds in a tree

1 2 **3** 4 5 6 7 8 9 10

this is 4~four

four windows in the door

1 2 3 **4** 5 6 7 8 9 10

this is 5~five

five bees round
the hive

1 2 3 4 5 6 7 8 9 10

this is 6~six

six fluffy chicks

1 2 3 4 5 6 7 8 9 10

this is 7~seven

there are seven days in a week

1 2 3 4 5 6 7 8 9 10

this is 8~eight

eight bars in the gate

1 2 3 4 5 6 7 8 9 10

this is 9~nine

nine trees in a line

1 2 3 4 5 6 7 8 9 10

this is 10~ten

ten chicks and a hen

2 3 4 5 6 7 8 9 10

this is 11~eleven

eleven musical
instruments

11 12 13 14 15 16 17 18 19 20

this is 12~twelve

there are twelve months
in a year

January	July
February	August
March	September
April	October
May	November
June	December

11 12 13 14 15 16 17 18 19 20

this is 13~thirteen

can you count thirteen ducks on the pond?

11 12 13 14 15 16 17 18 19 20

this is 14~fourteen

here are fourteen children

four in this row—4

and ten in this row—10

4+10=14

11 12 13 **14** 15 16 17 18 19 20

this is 15~fifteen

here are fifteen cats

eight in this row–8

and seven in this row–7

8+7=15

11 12 13 14 15 16 17 18 19 20

this is 16~sixteen

here are sixteen lollies

ten in this row–10

and six in this row–6

10+6=16

11 12 13 14 15 16 17 18 19 20

this is 17~seventeen

here are seventeen flowers

eight in this row-8

and nine in this row-9

8+9=17

11 12 13 14 15 16 17 18 19 20

this is 18~eighteen

here are eighteen socks

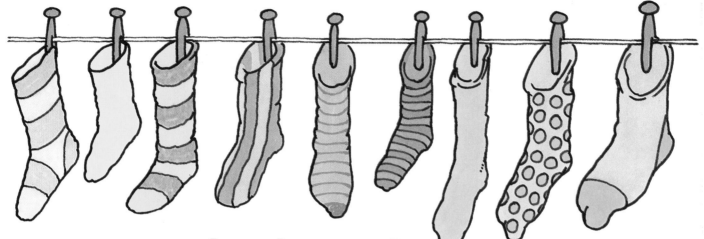

nine on this line-9

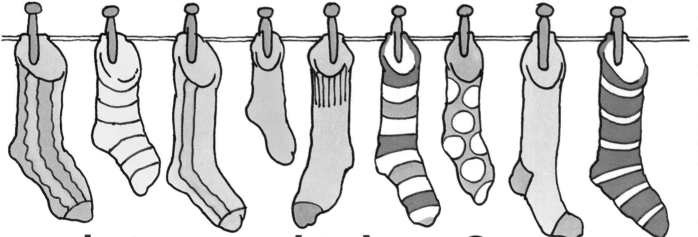

and nine on this line-9

9+9=18

11 12 13 14 15 16 17 18 19 20

this is 19 ~ nineteen

here are nineteen pencils

ten in this row-10

and nine in this row-9

10+9=19

11 12 13 14 15 16 17 18 19 20

this is 20~twenty

here are twenty bottles

ten in this row-10

and ten in this row

10+10=20

11 12 13 14 15 16 17 18 19 20

this is 30~thirty

thirty is three tens,
can you count 30 candles
on the cake?

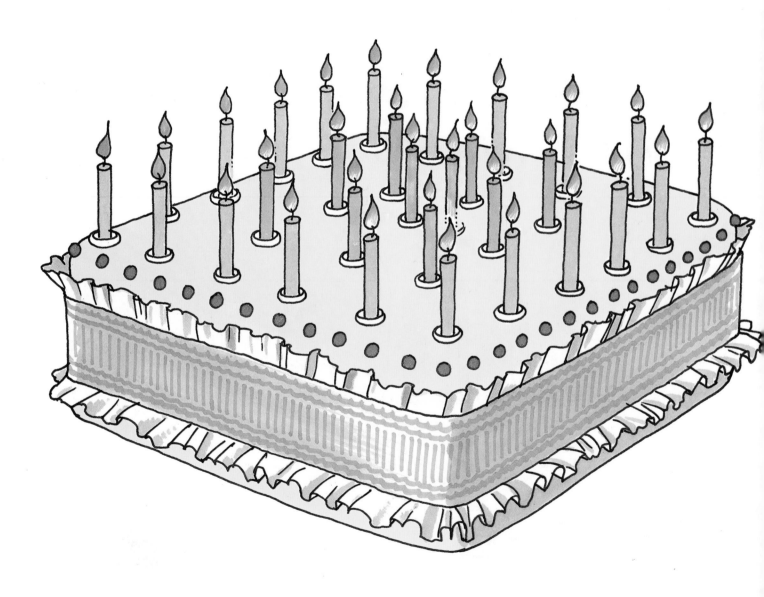

10 20 **30** **40** 50

this is 40~forty

forty is four tens,
can you count 40 apples
on this tree?

60 70 80 90 100

this is 50 ~ fifty

fifty is five tens, can you count 50 stones in the river?

10 20 30 40 50

this is 60~sixty

sixty is six tens,
can you count 60 minutes
on the clock?

60 70 80 90 100

this is 70~seventy

seventy is seven tens,
can you add up all the fruit
to make 70?

10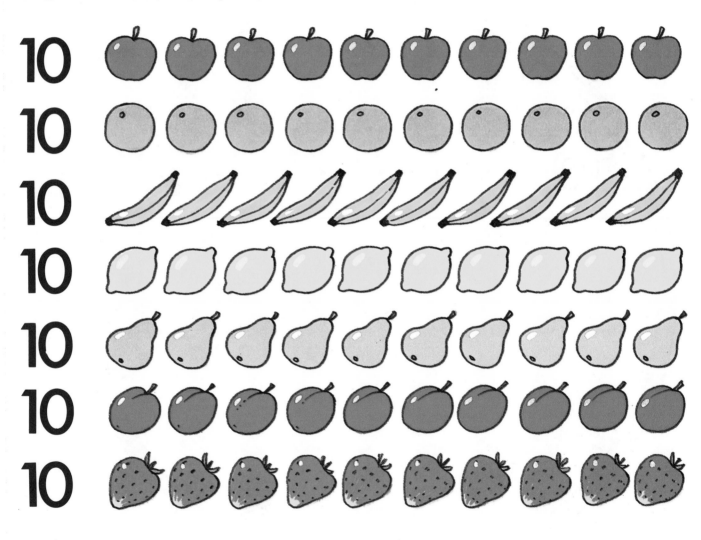
10
10
10
10
10
10

10 20 30 40 50

this is 80~eighty

eighty is eight tens,
can you add up all the objects
to make 80?

10
10
10
10
10
10
10
10

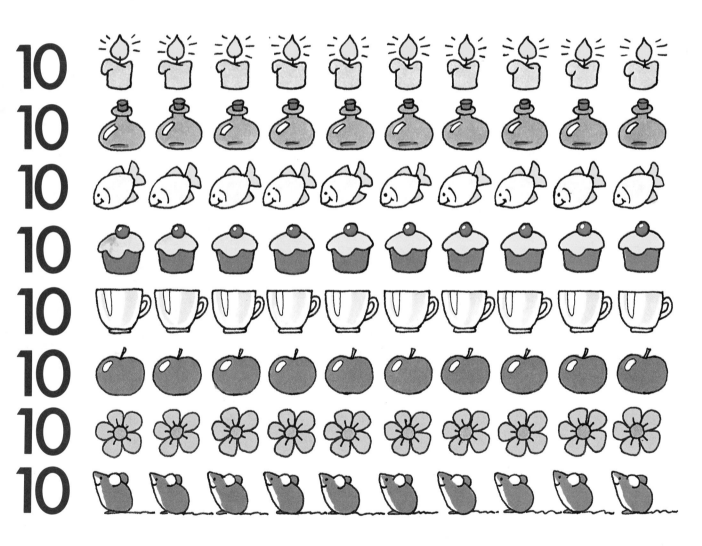

60 70 80 90 100

this is 90 ~ ninety

ninety is nine tens,
can you add up all the objects
to make 90?

10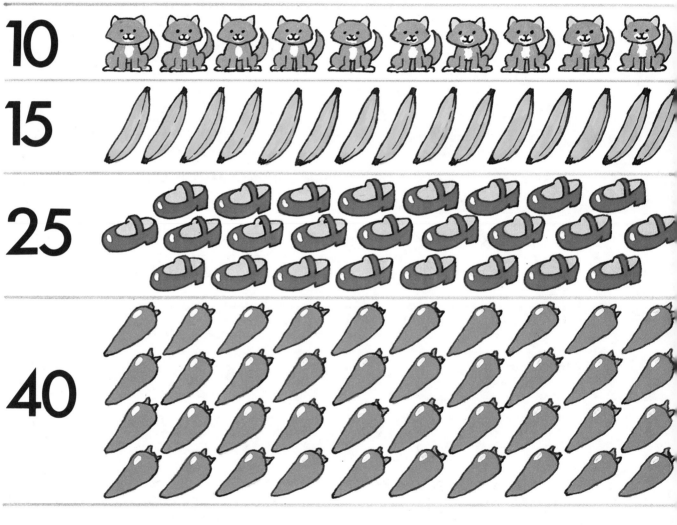

15

25

40

10 20 30 40 50

this is 100~hundred

one hundred is ten tens,
can you add up these numbers
to make 100?

ten _____ 10
fifteen _____ 15
twenty _____ 20
twenty five _____ 25
thirty _____ 30

_____
_____

well done!

60 70 80 90 100

my first book of
TELLING THE TIME

On the clock face the long hand points to the minutes, the short hand points to the hour. Sometimes on clocks and watches there is another hand which goes round the face very quickly, it is called the second hand.

There are 60 seconds in a minute.
A second is as quick as a wink.

There are 60 minutes in an hour.

There are two types of clock, one with a face and hands, and one that just has numbers called digits. Some digital clocks show 12 hours, others show the full 24 hours in a day.

This is 2 o'clock in the afternoon on a 12 hour clock.

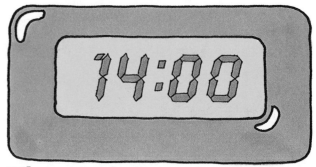

This is the same time on a 24 hour clock.

These clocks show all 24 hours in a day.
The time from 12 midnight to 12 noon is called
'A.M.'. From noon to midnight is called 'P.M.'.

At 12 noon, the 12 hour clocks start to go
round again. The 24 hour clocks just go on
adding up to 24.

At 12 midnight a new day begins, and all the
clocks start again.

Here is a story about an exciting day out.
Learn about time from the little clocks
in each picture.

The twins are fast
asleep. It is 7 o'clock.

Here comes the milkman. It is 7.15, a quarter past seven.

7:15

Here comes the postman with the letters and a parcel. It is 7.30, half past seven.

7:30

Mother calls: "Get up, it's late, it is 8 o'clock. We are going out today."

The twins jump out of bed and run to the bathroom to get washed.

Hurry up twins, get dressed straight away. Pull on your socks, put on your shoes, it is 8.15, a quarter past eight.

Breakfast is on the table ready to eat. It is 8.30, half past eight.

"Grab your coats, I will lock the door. The bus will be here at 9 o'clock," says mother.

They get to the bus stop out of breath. Here comes the bus, right on time.

"Where are we going?" ask the twins. Mother says: "Wait and see." The bus stops at the railway station at 9.15, a quarter past nine.

The train arrives at 9.30, half past nine by the station clock. Climb aboard, and off we go.

The train speeds on through the countryside, past woods and fields and over bridges. Half an hour goes by. It is now 10 o'clock.

At last the train stops at a little station and everyone gets off.

The ticket collector has a big watch that says 10.15, a quarter past ten.

The twins and their mother leave the station and start walking down the lane.

It was a lovely walk
down the lanes, through
a village, and past a
church with a clock
that said 10.45,
a quarter to eleven.

"Here we are at last," says mother. It is
a park with lots of animals. "We open at
11 o'clock," says the man at the
gate, "you're just on time."

First they see a hippo.

Then a zebra with lots of stripes.

They make friends with a monkey...

...but not with the camel.

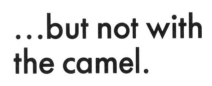

Then it was 11.45, a quarter to twelve. "Come on," says mother, "there's something I want you to see."

The keeper is feeding the
sea lions at 12 o'clock.

At 12.30, half past twelve, he feeds
the penguins with fish from a
bucket, and the twins help him.

"Look! It's 1 o'clock," says mother. "It's our feeding time now. We will have a picnic at that table over there."

It is afternoon. The 24 hour clock now says 13.00, the thirteenth hour of the day.

Mother says: "It is 1.30, half past one.
I will sit here and you can look around
for an hour by yourselves."

First the twins go
to see the parrots and
the other lovely birds.

At 2 o'clock they go to Pets Corner to play with the baby animals.

When they get back to mother, she says:
"You are just in time to see the dolphins at
2.30, half past two."

"Oh dear," say the twins, looking at their watches. "It is 3 o'clock and there is still so much to see."

They see a big brown bear.

A tiger that growls at them.

And a lion that is fast asleep.

They see a giraffe, as tall as a house...

...and a big bad tempered rhino.

4:30 16:30

"Have we time to see the snakes and the crocodiles?" ask the twins. "Yes," says mother. "If we are finished by 5 o'clock.

"You two must be hungry," says mother. "We have time for a quick snack before we leave for home."

When everyone has finished eating, the clock says 5.30, half past five.

"Now we must hurry to the gates," says mother. "The park closes at 6 o'clock."

"Goodbye," says the man at the gate. "I hope you have enjoyed your visit."

6:00   18:00

They get back to the station at 6.45, a quarter to seven. Mother says: "We have to wait 15 minutes for the 7 o'clock train."

6:45   18:45

Here it comes, right on time.

7:00   19:00

After their journey by train and bus
they arrive home at 8 o'clock just as
it is getting dark.

  8:00  20:00

The twins go straight upstairs to get washed and ready for bed.

Mother brought them a hot drink. "You must be tired," she says. "It is 8.30, half past eight."

By 9 o'clock they are both fast asleep. It has been a long busy day!

9:00   21:00

The twins are asleep, but the clocks go on counting the time up to 12 o'clock midnight.

10:00 22:00   11:00 23:00   12:00 24:00

Can you fill in the missing times from these clocks?

7:30   :   8:45   :

10:00   :   11:30   :

12:15   :   3:00   4:45

my first rhyming picture abc

A a

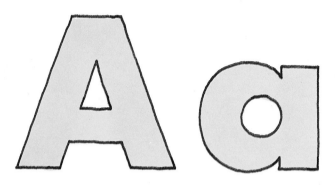

a is for apples
some green, some red

a is for aeroplane
that flies overhead

a is for apricot
that grows on a tree

a is for adding
one, two, three

B b

b is for baker
who bakes crusty bread

b is for blanket
that covers your bed

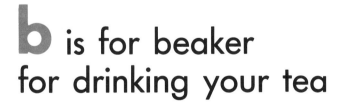

b is for beaker
for drinking your tea

b is for binoculars
for miles you can see

C c

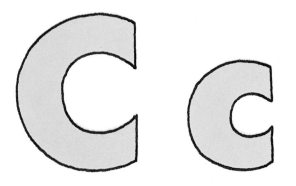

C is for cat
with its whiskers long

C is for cart
pulled by a horse so strong

C is for carrot
crunchy and sweet

C is for cars
that you see in the street

D d

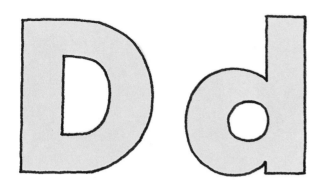

d is for dancing
so light on your feet

d is for drinking
orange juice so sweet

d is for dog
wagging his tail

d is for dinghy
with a bright blue sail

E e

e is for eggs
see the chicks that hatch out

e is for excitement
when we all laugh and shout

e is for elephant
so gentle but strong

e is for ending
the show with a song!

F f

f is for farm
with fresh milk and cheese

f is for fingers
the toothpaste to squeeze

f is for fan
a cool breeze to make

f is for fish
that swim in the lake

G g

g is for grapes
some green, some black

g is for garbage
that's put in a sack

g is for garden
where flowers do grow

g is for gumboots
to wear in the snow

H h

h is for hedgehog
who cleans up the garden

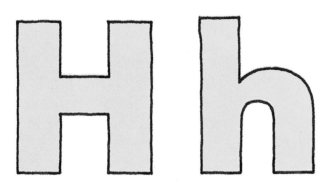

h is for hiccup
I beg your pardon!

h is for hymn
that is sung in a church

h is for hen
asleep on her perch

I i

i is for island
surrounded by sea

i is for iguana
a lizard you see

i is for inn
a welcoming sight

The Sun

i is for ivory
so smooth and so white

J j

J is for jug
full of water so cool

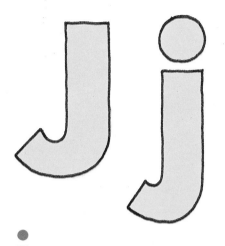

j is for jumping
into the pool

j is for jam
to spread on your bread

j is for jet
that roars overhead

K k

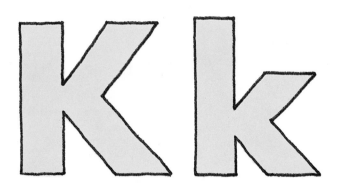

k is for king
so stately and tall

k is for kitten
who plays with the ball

k is for kitchen
where cooking is done

k is for keeping
a secret, it's fun

L l

l is for lion
so noble and strong

l is for the lark
and merry birdsong

l is for leopard
known for his spots

l is for lemon
to squeeze lots and lots

M m

m is for mouse
who lives in a barn

m is for minstrel
who sings his own yarn

m is for mask
that hides your face

25miles

m is for marathon
a very long race

N n

n is for nurse
so patient with care

n is for nightingale
with its song so rare

n is for nut
so crunchy to eat

n is for navy
and ships in the fleet

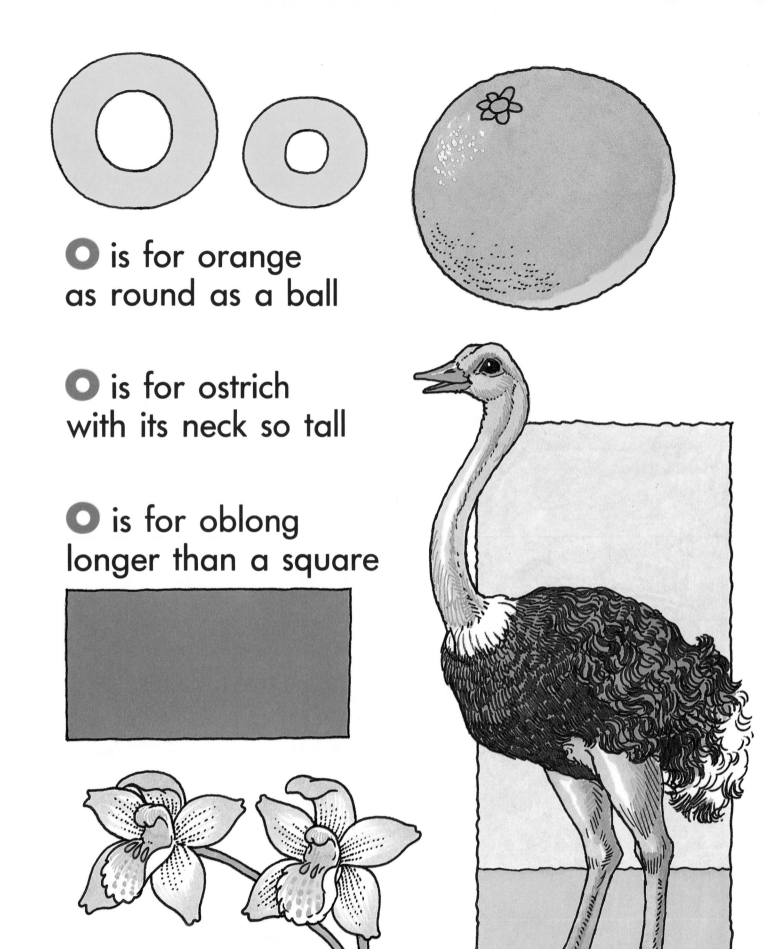

O is for orange
as round as a ball

O is for ostrich
with its neck so tall

O is for oblong
longer than a square

O is for orchid
a flower so rare

P p

p is for parrot
a beautiful bird

p is for pasture
and grazing a herd

p is for parachute
that floats to the ground

p is for pumpkin
oval or round

Qq

q is for quack
it's the way a duck talks

q is for queen
who smiles as she walks

q is for quilt
so warm yet so light

q is for quail
in migratory flight

R r

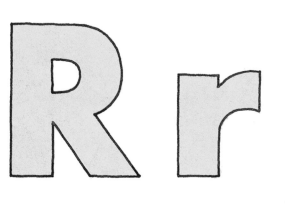

r is for robin
with its bright red breast

r is for rook
high in his nest

r is for roses
that grow down the lane

r is for rainbow
after the rain

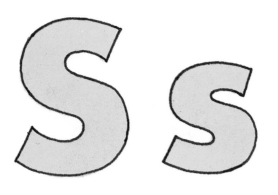

S is for sparrow
to the garden he comes

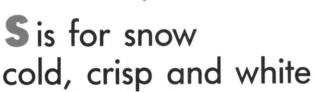

S is for starling
looking for crumbs

S is for snow
cold, crisp and white

S is for stars
that shine in the night

T t

t is for target
at which we take aim

t is for teddybear
he's good for a game

t is for ticket
to ride on the train

t is for tea-time
it's jelly again!

U is for universe
the planets and stars

U is for Uranus
a planet, like Mars

U is for uniforms
the guards in a row

U is for under
the arches we go!

V v

V is for vine
heavy with fruit

V is for valet
preparing a suit

V is for vikings
who sailed the high seas

V is for vegetables
potatoes, parsnips and peas

Ww

W is for water
we use to make tea

W is for whale
that swims in the sea

W is for the willow
that grows by the stream

W is for waking
from a beautiful dream

X x

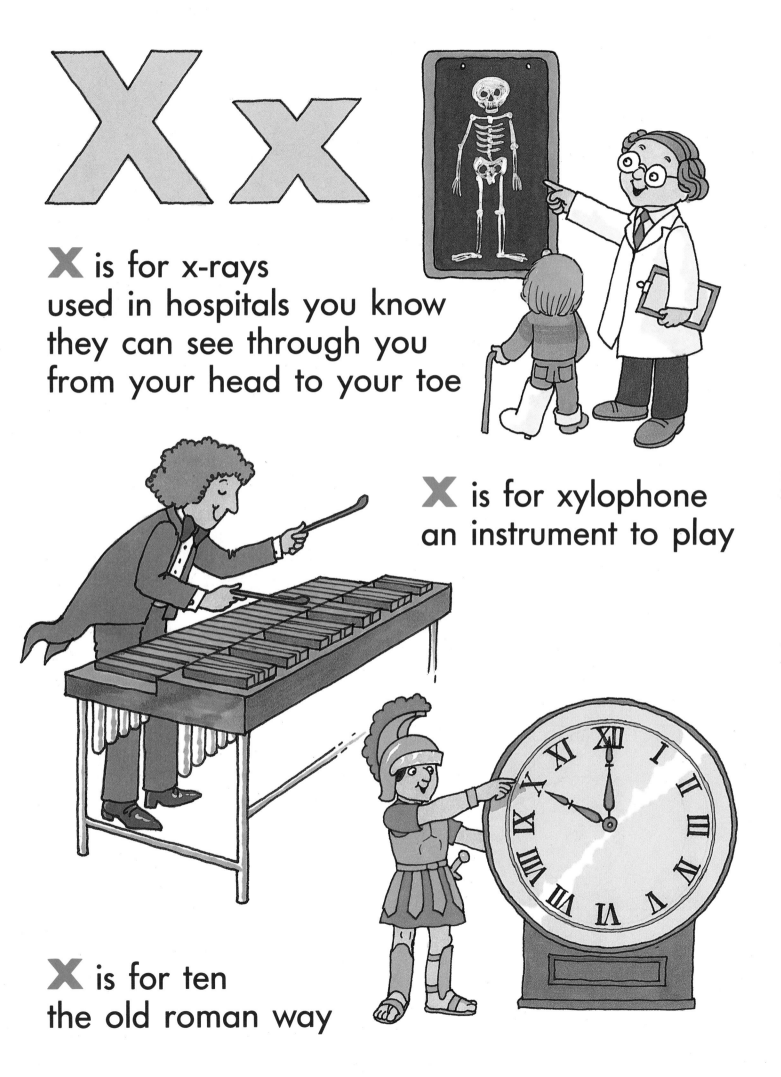

X is for x-rays
used in hospitals you know
they can see through you
from your head to your toe

X is for xylophone
an instrument to play

X is for ten
the old roman way

Y y

y is for yellow
and daffodils so pale

y is for yacht
under full sail

y is for yeast
that helps make bread dough

y is for yearling
a young horse you know

Z z

Z is for zebras
with their black and white coats

Z is for zither
playing musical notes

Z is for zoo
and the animals there

Z is for zig-zag
in a car beware